DA

A Slice of Snow

By Joan Walsh Anglund

A
Slice of
Snow

A
Book
of
Poems
by
Joan Walsh Anglund

Harcourt Brace Jovanovich, Inc., New York

First edition
ISBN 0-15-183015-0
Library of Congress Catalog Card Number: 70-118830
Printed in the United States of America

Peace is the harvest of love
as
War is the fruit of hate.

For
every
murder
I
allow,

        I
       am
    the victim.

Spring
        does
        not
        ask
an
audience,
            but
            shapes
            each
            blossom
            perfectly,
                    indifferent
                    to
                    applause.

The miracle is
        that life continues.
The sorrow is
        that we do not.

Child,

who sculptured you,

that

your

face

is

so

like

mine

and

yet

so

much

your

own?

Like brothers at play,
 Doubt and Belief
  forever teeter-totter
   within my soul.

On
the thin line
between dawn
and darkness,
Sunrise
writes
her
poem.

Self
　　forever paints
　　　　　　her own portrait
　　across
　　　　the wide canvas
　　　　　　　　of Life.

Be careful
        which dream
                you clutch . . .

for dreams come true!

Doubt did the cutting,
Hate was the knife.
There was only one thrust,
    but it severed a life.

If you love me,

        you will remember.

If you do not,

        it is better

                that we both forget.

Where is the yesterday
          that worried us so?

The arrow
        of ambition
                flies high,
but,
     missing target,
           is deadly
               in descent.

Memory
         has many hollows. . .

    Let me hide
         in one.

Like greedy fish,
  we bob to the surface
    when crumbs of praise
      are tossed.

Do not be sad
        that you have suffered,

Be glad
        that you have lived.

What need we teach a child . . .
    with our books and rules?

Let him walk among the hills and flowers,
    let him gaze upon the waters,
        let him look up to the stars . . .

        and he will have his wisdom.

How cold
            is Conclusion
        when
            Beginning
                    was
                        so
                            warm.

Home!
        Bring them home,
                these children dead.

Above each head
        we nail a cross.

        Oh . . . heavy cost!
        On children lost,
                the beast of war
                        is
                        fed.

My mind
        never tells me. . . .

Only the mirror speaks
           of the passing years.

One rose
　　　　given in love
is remembered more
　　　　than roomfuls
　　　　　　　　given in duty.

It is not I

        who speaks,

    but Life

        within me

            who has much to say!

What matters?
> Very little.

Only . . .
> the flicker of light
> > within the darkness,

> the feeling of warmth
> > within the cold,

> the knowledge of love
> > within the void.

When ideas

        are

           narrow,

    they

       become

          the bars

by

which

    a

    man

    is

       imprisoned.

How easy
                the breath
                        that kills a flame.

How hard
            to kindle
                    that light again.

Cold words kill
                and
                        kind words kindle.

By words withheld,

                    a dream may dwindle.

It is when
        we earn love
                least
    that
      we need it
           most.

So often, that which we are
    is sacrificed
        to that
            which we wish
                ourselves
                    to be.

We are separate stars
    within
        a mutual night.

Against the encompassing darkness,
    let us
        together
            light our candles.